laisha rosnau

PLUCK

 **NIGHTWOOD EDITIONS**

2014

Nightwood Editions
P.O. Box 1779
Gibsons, BC V0N 1V0
Canada
www.nightwoodeditions.com

Nightwood Editions acknowledges financial support from the Government
of Canada through the Canada Book Fund and the Canada Council for the Arts,
and from the Province of British Columbia through the British Columbia Arts
Council and the Book Publisher's Tax Credit.

Cover Design: Carleton Wilson
Typesetting: Angela Caravan

Library and Archives Canada Cataloguing in Publication

Rosnau, Laisha, 1972-, author
Pluck / Laisha Rosnau.

Poems.
ISBN 978-0-88971-295-9 (pbk.)
Printed in Canada

I. Title.

PS8585.O8336P58 2014   C811'.6   C2014-900623-3

For Jonah and Amalia

CONTENTS

FISSURE & FLOOD

THAT FEELING

We're now in the glory of not knowing what we're doing. Though prolonged falling gathers fatigue, even into winter. After the rain, more rain. I've never thought my guts would shake with echoes while I declare my love.

—Rosemarie Waldrop

FISSURE & FLOOD

TO DO:

1) Diminish fear's pretense of famine

2) Act as though you're fine with growth's weak stems; become scandent and twine or creep along a surface for support

3) Tackle lucidity with digests of the roughed-in, illusory; rub them until they blend

4) Finger dread, tickle the hem of the unfounded, remain groundless in your anxieties

5) Clamber to the lip of the rise, rimmed in last light, but don't think you'll reach it before dark—or ever, really

6) Shelter pages, craft ports from folio, fold, stich, crack spines, open

7) Cast doubts like line, be fine with the shrug, the wince, the enviable

8) Traipse through each season's unabashed way with itself, wallow in the riches it tosses aside

9) Teem with florid hopes, bankroll folly, toss slights to cynics

10) Bend to accommodate rhythm

11) Shed desire out back, bring it in with the wood, light it up, trail the house with shards, revel in splinters, smart with it all

12) Adopt the vernacular of one constantly agape

FISSURE & FLOOD

Little fish, big fish, swimming in the water,
Come back here & give me my daughter.
—PJ Harvey/traditional

Whatever you do, don't picture a tight-mouthed
sergeant demanding you push so hard that you launch

round offspring into the cut-banks that girdle the city. Don't
    think of salmon swimming upstream,

bloody and ragged, hooked on the confluence;
how the current forms clouds out of streaks of blood.

Instead, imagine women. They are everywhere, scrubbed
and name-tagged or walking the streets, legs thin as pins,

heels into each day like a the needle in your arm, saline drip
    to replace what the baby will pull from you.

They'll beat pans to flush those babies out
as a bear looks up from the dumpster behind the hospital,

waves its snout in wide rhythmic arcs,
    a priest swinging incense.

The space between vein and blood is all there is
between you and her,
               and then there is more—

❀

Each time I give birth, my husband waters the garden
in response, plumps the front yard with pots of tomatoes

as I turn myself inside out, reveal
        how rosy we all are —our skin, theirs.

FAIRYTALES FOR LOSS

Once upon a time there was a fawn writhing
in pain on our back lawn. Spooked by us,
it hobbled off, left a message: grow up, cope.

An example of what grown-ups do:
rinse the dishes, shake their hands,
summon their spouse, wonder

what else to do about the deer
struggling on the grass.
Calls might be made to others,

advice sought, but adulthood allows
for as many or as few shards of wisdom
to be followed; permits wildlife,

injured and thrashing, to remain
on the property until it dies.
Truth is, we weren't callous—

even with a broken leg, the deer could move
quickly enough that it seemed fleeting,
as though a figment of damage.

We had hoped that movement
would take it farther than the copse
at the lake's edge where it stopped.

Will you remember when we buried it,
how you wished for the fawn a return
to life unharmed? Not likely—

your childhood will become a fable
and it won't so much be your innocence
that disappears as our guard over it;

the mother I am to you now will be gone,
just as the doe eventually stopped coming
once we buried her young.

PLUCK

1.

Get married at seventeen, maybe
eighteen, don't smile
for the camera, look
stoic instead. This may take

some endurance, after all. Have one
child, then two or three more
in quick succession. Just when
it seems like propagation

isn't a question, stain your sheets
red, ask yourself why, why now,
then lose another at a year old.
Take to the field — there's land

to clear, by hand if necessary,
not much time to wonder why
about anything. Come down
with something in midlife,

shake, quake and crumble
with it then take the doctor's word,
have another child, this one
prescribed as a cure. Don't wonder

why she, in all her round health,
is neither a pill nor anything
that can placate you. Keep
roaring, keep laughing,

prop yourself up on your walker,
later roll your wheelchair through days
until they become years.
When he dies, they think you will

go soon after. Instead live longer
than most, your hospital room becoming
your kitchen back home. Laugh when they
don't know that everything has its place.

2.

Wait, wait for
marriage, though it may be
unfashionable to do so at your age,
in your age, it will

age you, anyway.
When you do marry, don't
think of it as something
you've either succumbed to

or claimed victory over. Accept
everything with grace, keep on
the reserved side, even after seven
children crowd your body, your home,

three bedrooms—one for girls, one for boys,
your own shared only with him. Despite
cries and quarrels, never relent
to the ways they want in.

Keep yourself to yourself
as you give and give and give
and then say goodbye
to each of them as they leave.

Open books in their absence, read
as much and as long as you want.
After you are gone, your husband will write
a memoir, note your nervous

breakdown, as though that's the only
term for it—and, really,
what else could he call it?
Don't go lightly, tear

the feeding tube out. Be remembered
for how lovely you were, how kind,
how no one knew how sick your body was
because your mind never forgot anything.

3.

Oh, good Lord, forget
about marriage, friends tell you,
it's a new era, but not
for you, you won't give

anything away until you loop
your name into the registry, sign away
both last name and girlhood religion,
take a new one of each.

The priest won't be swinging
his incense over you any more,
though you smell its cloying smoke
your entire honeymoon in San Francisco.

Look, you can be hip,
you can be the proud owner
of one of Alberta's first truck-campers,
you can take to the open road

then move with your beatnik
across the country, make feeble attempts
to speak French before the province revolts,
names you and your kind a subversion.

Refuse immersion for your kids,
decide to leave, be alienated by them
on your own turf. Move west yet recoil
from the coast, choose a shallow valley,

water more still, pooled in lakes.
Cultivate everything around you
and get the kids to pick, prune and harvest
as you go. Dig, fertilize, and preserve

then sand, refinish and paint
as though the world can be remade,
if not in your likeness then one
that you like.

4.

Move in with him, why
not? Wonder why your mother
is upset, why she will not
meet his eyes. When the snow hits

the city and he leaves
to go home for Christmas, quit
your job without telling anyone.
Stay in except to make tracks

to the corner store and back for cola,
milk and Froot Loops. Live
on that until you too go
home, pretend to be fine.

Try to teach your mom
how to inhale. Wait a few years
then move in with another man.
Watch how your mom flirts,

what you've taught her, perhaps.
Live lean and live with him
for years and when you cheat
and he leaves, be indignant,

desperate. Wait,
learn a few things, or believe
that you have, become more cocky
than you need to be.

When you meet him, be wary,
Tell yourself he'll never change,

he's not a project, you're not
that into him, but then he gets in

and you egg him on until both of you
say yes then branch out together
and, my God, bear fruit, as though you're
a tree, rooted, fickle as seasons.

5.

Be born to a couple
of idealistic ideologues, listen
to them battle and banter
themselves silly, make them

laugh with the way you spin
circles, naked except for your boots,
eyes closed, hands raised as if
all girls, everywhere, can do this.

Be the embodiment of your grandmother's
curse when she asked for her daughter
a daughter like her own. Run headlong
and headstrong through that hex. Laugh.

Form allegiances with each of them —
mother, father, brother — take advantage
of whatever your wiles grant you.
Don't take for granted

anything your charms grant you, either.
Whatever you do, don't listen
to directives, especially not ones written
in a lame kind of pseudo verse.

Don't believe that anything can
be encapsulated. You aren't her
and she isn't any of the women
who have come before you.

We are all on our own here,
our knowledge plucked
from our own imaginings. Choose
your favourite fruit, take a bite.

ACCUMULATION

Dishes accumulate, laundry accumulates, toys accumulate, plastic
    accumulates
I can't acclimatize, you don't acclimatize, climate doesn't quite acclimatize
Sun hits the window, wind hits the window, hail hits the window
I hit you, you hit me, the kids hit each other, love hits us in the chest
Love demands us, patience demands us, endurance demands us, time
    demands us
Give us time, give you time, I give time, time gives the kids an advantage
This too shall pass, our past has passed, the kids fly past, I'll pass, thanks
Please me, you please, what pleases us, pleases them, again and again—yet
how can we please each other, do each other justice, just us,
we and us and you and me and all we've collected, accumulated
    amassed, a mess, amen—

EASY NOW

What I said about how easy this could be, how easy
I was once known to be? There was no truth
in that, no shortcuts, no high roads either.
We hitched a trailer to our car, coxed it north,
lived a few years then angled it south again,
two kids strapped into the back, cat in a cage.

At the motel, one of us wrestles the cat
down from the curtains, the other wakes
the owner for buckets of ice to soothe fevers,
road-induced, small bodies racked with change.
We're all too tired, too hot or too hungry
but we're fine. Let's go. We're on our way.

Easy now, Sweetheart, when I said it won't be long,
we'll be there soon, I meant it figuratively,
and the figure I meant to stand in was Christ-like,
an epiphany of patience and understanding.
We, however, barely have a handle
on table manners or bedtimes

or how many hours it takes to rot a mind
in front of a screen. We call each other Dude,
as it suits some of us, some of the time,
and that's all we can expect from family. It's easy,
really. Let's all put on clean pants. Let's go
east instead, toward high plains and badlands,

the urge to exhume dinosaur fossils so we can
exclaim, *Hey, look, we're still young!* Or remember
a time when your own childhood family
collected maps printed on paper placemats
from Husky diners. Can we find some
of those now? Please, please say we can.
Easy, slow down. They've both fallen asleep.

THE KIND OF WEATHER I HAVE

The pygmy nuthatches struck
up this morning with a pine leeched
by beetles and summer's hot past.

They darted in and out of one hole,
as though all the same bird, endlessly
repeating, then took flight,

veered so close to the window,
said, *come on now, come out, it's not over yet.*
I tell them, you don't know winter,

the kind I have—the weather always
unreasonable, strange in some way, either balking
with shoots of green in February (sneaky teasers)

or all bluster and show, graffitiying
windows with frost, siphoning
barren light into rooms.

✿

Today, late autumn sun's half-witted,
taunted by clouds hopped up with rain
just waiting to let go, take a swipe at me

(that fight, a face full of vodka and ice.)
Each season is both familiar and a surprise,
like old boyfriends returning. I'll concede

to the house, where nothing is more real
than memory; the present an oddity, wedded
to me without being gilded with nostalgia.

A sharp-shinned hawk dives and a bird hits
the pane behind my chair. I go outside
to see the damage but it's only feathers.

The larger bird will eat the smaller
elsewhere and I'll find
nothing, not even in spring.

AMONG APOLOGIES

The bears are congregating again, all brazen
and sashaying, no sheepish back ends around here.

They burgeon from two and then three and then four, roll
in birdseed, lollygag in every sightline.

I imagine they multiply overnight,
accretion of fur as they mushroom the front lawn,

rank steam rising off them when they rumble awake,
take over the property. Before we go outside, we yell

out screened windows, then roar through
open doors. If that doesn't do it, we've collected rocks

that the kids place in my palms, and stand back as I lob
them, pelt their coats. I feel like apologizing but, seriously,

these bears are too comfortable. At night once the kids
are asleep, I sit on the front porch, sip Amaretto,

light clove cigarettes, wear a headlamp so I can flip
through magazines while the bears snuffle

the loam, smash snouts through understory as I listen, dumb,
and dog-ear the pages that I'll rip out in the morning,

scatter throughout house until I feel sorry that I haven't
done enough to make our lives a photo shoot.

Drink and smoke gone, I shout to the sounds of unseen bears, tell them that I know they're there; sometimes shadows hold more than darkness.

One morning, the sunrise will flare green and I'll know it's a sign. By then, the bears will have moved on.

SHAME, REVISITED

Other people do it better, I'm sure.
These kids requiring costumes, gifts,
something like talent, balanced just so.

These kids are costing me some nights
of sleep, some sense of mid-level sanity.
Other people do it better, I'm sure,

but they seem to love me for it, or despite.
I manage crafts, pumpkins, candy—consumption
something like talent, balanced just so—

then the party we go to puts me to shame,
lanterns slung through trees, witches cackling,
"Other people do it better." I'm sure

I'll feel okay with a drink in my hand. My baby
lion roars around the party, unsteady, showing
something like talent, balanced just so.

I hope for her so much more than a cat costume
unpeeled, cold skin against a vinyl seat, thinking,
Other people do this better, I'm sure.

Sweetheart, don't reveal too much, too early
or remembering will become the same as to forget,
something like a talent, balanced just so.

MUSIC BOX DANCER

That summer was humid—
heat hiccupped off the lake,
wallpaper peeled from walls
and that boy held us hostage
in his backyard. What was his name,
again? He was older, perhaps
even nine, and he corralled everyone
younger than him, sat us in rows
of lawn chairs, smelled the lick of fear
as dense as heat stuck to us. What games
did he play to slowly allow one child
after another go free? I have no memory
of that, just of the two of us, the last
ones stuck to chairs, the shriek
of cicadas and the song of the piano
composer next door tumbling over
the thrill of sweet new chords.

WE WERE REASONING WILDLY

What is reasonable art
to hang above one's marriage
bed? You thought shelter—an image

of a cabin glowing in snowy woods,
the oil paint thick and ridged, the frame
white, a little campy. We found it

in the basement along with other things.
The wire to hang it seemed sturdy
then busted one day but it didn't crash

down, instead balanced on the headboard.
You suggested we repair it
but I prefer to stumble

on objects whole, hope
all remains intact.
Back in the basement,

I found two paintings of owls, one snowy,
one great horned, perched on forked branches,
each looking either stoic or calm or both.

I hung the white one over my head, the one
with horned tufts over yours. Not to be too symbolic
but there are reasons to hang wild things

over us, two birds in different frames
on the same wall. So many reasons, one
being we should call out in the night more often.

A real owl, counterpart to your painting, startles
us out of sleep and we roll into each other,
lap at the heat of our paired skin, then dive

into our own worlds of sleep, talons out, ready
to plunder the whorled nests that will feed us,
keep us flying, silently toward each other.

SLIGHTLY CREEPY CAMPING SITE

That's not a tent, not really,
just a canvas tarp propped
and sagging between two poles.

There is no floor, no sleeping
bag. She reclines on a bent
arm, legs swung out

in front of her, an empty
canoe mirrored on the lake,
the outline of others

still there—a trick
of shading or memory.
The trees are leafless and yet

she'll lounge in a ribbed undershirt
and panties until you stop
wondering why she's there.

BOY SCOUTS

There are five boys in a row and the one partially hidden
behind another looks the strangest. Only one of his eyes
is visible, brow raised, though the other boys
look none too friendly, either.

They are just boys, in uniforms, caps, knee socks.
Each holds his body differently — arms stiff
or loosely clasped, hands folded or knuckles
knocked up against one another.

Oh, and their little Boy Scout ties. Only one
wears glasses — he also has an eye patch,
the brightest smudge of white where all else
is shaded red and gold. The long grass at their feet

is yellow and something else is there, perhaps
a bag, wine-coloured. Beside that, one shoe, high-heeled,
the pump once as white as that eye patch, now
scuffed brown. The sky. That sky is maraschino red.

FRAME

There is no way I am going to scurry
across the rock face that rises from this lake
like you do, so I'll wade around it,
though I know my bones
will ache clear through my skin.
It will be good—you've promised me—
the carcass and rotting meat of an elk
that must have fallen before the first snow,
preserved until the thaw. I'll like it,
you say, the way it disembodies
impermanence, how the cold can stop
and start the process, freeze-frame
      the body between,
        make winter timeless.

You drop into the deepest baritone,
tell me you will take the finest bone,
clean and dry and pointed, and press it
against the wet arch of my foot
until beads of blood appear
like small berries in spring—
then we'll laugh and joke about Christ
and poetry and bloodletting.
We're too cold or not clever enough,
the elk isn't where you remembered it,
and before we can figure out
which jokes work, what stanzas might form,
      there is rock and water
        and our ragged sense of time.

Much later, I imagine the elk
as it watches us through the trees.
It doesn't move until we leave
then shakes off the last snow,
lifts its hooves
          high over deadfall,
          moves inland.

MIND THE DEVOTION

the mallow nine bark yields too much,
litters sky,

branch and grass alike
with bloom after bloom after bloody pink

bloom, multiplied on each other, this beauty
bush, I've heard it called.

my words a struggle, sparse,
lured, over

and over; mind the devotion—
we're both at it, the tree and I, we shed

pretty things, our bark peeling beneath.

✿

our multiple lives taunt us,
in turns brash—like the two

phone lines strung through
our house, tolling, imploring—

or discreet, choices tucked away,
undergarments, folded

into bedding and stacked
in the closet, discovered only

when a sheet is shaken,
swells like a parachute,

and panties float to the ground.

*

paired, we painted
bright pink side by side

with electric orange,
divvied the room with acidic sunset,

someone's Seventies dreamscape,
and it closed in on us,

twilight and pot smoke and then
darkness, but never

a kiss, nothing
more. we didn't end

up together, he and I.

*

at eighty, they share one
parking space at the hospital,

their Harleys side by side.
visiting the maternity ward,

he is knocked for six
by new skin and that's it—

he leaves alone, wants more
sex, he tells her later.

can you believe it? she asks.
Jesus, she says.

yes, no, Jesus is right.

❋

we fret over electricity, house plants,
chance rejected and re-invited

government sponsored
radio keeps us current,

lets us keep our own company
included in the conversation.

we listen while we peel oranges
in unbroken spirals,

prop the skin up
so it appears to be full,

then ground the fruit to juice.

✿

they bear more than
likeness to us, those two

icons of our wooing, our pledge.
our birthdays all garland

a three week period
of the calendar and we mark

another year as ours, as his,
as hers, as yours, as mine, as ours

again, the hours of our inner worlds,
the chicanery of time,

spinning the clock like a top.

AN AFFRONT

In the cafe, two men talk about their grown daughters,
how their new babies change everything, now
as they did back then. They debate
serotonin and big pharma and complicity.
Their own baby girls fledged, mouths and throats
their own to fill and swallow, the men still offer
each other suggestions.

If they ask for my thoughts, I will tell them
that all these years I've been mistaking
swallowtails for monarchs. Now I wonder
what I drove into — wings folded, they looked like shoots
on a dirt road until I steered into them and they rose,
hailed the windshield with gold and black.
Some didn't have the chance,
their flight flattened under tires.

They don't ask. One man asserts:
*Semantics or not, I'm fussy
about the word philosophy.*

Listen, babies are an affront and a confirmation
of time's trickery at once. That doesn't mean
I should keep pushing them out of me, ripe
with contradiction, does it? That's no philosophy
to live by, is it? Perhaps I should ask these two,
full of ideals, nostalgic for the drugs of their past.

An artists speaks on the radio and we all listen
as he tells us that he will not make any more boring art.
The men tire of their own chatter and now one reads
a book about coming off anti-depressants.

I was going to spin a gossamer metaphor
about cocoons or butterflies. Forget it.
I will not write any more boring poems.

OLD NEWS

Some lady is looking for old bras on Craigslist. She talks about
leaning over and pouring herself into rockets on the radio.
Like I listen. This is my mother's radio station. *Bam!* My phone
goes off. Our phones are smarter than we are.

The news is: she's been gang-raped, I've been gang-raped,
you've been gang-raped, blah de blah de blah. We're all part
of the story. How you feeling? Sore? My bra
keeps digging into me. Man, this is old news.

Lady, I'm too young for this. Wait — Instagram my ass!
No, really! I mean, take a photo of my ass and I'll post it,
maybe pin me some tail. They don't get our sense of humour.
Hey, don't tickle me! I'm serious.

I babysat for her once. Her son's kind of quiet, really sweet.
Her daughter, though? She's cute but she's crazy.
She wouldn't shut up. The dad's not bad, for an old guy,
but don't get a ride home with him alone. We've heard girls

charge him up. We've heard he's been charged for that.
He won't touch us, though. We've heard the news today, oh boy,
and my mom says I don't know anything about the real world, that history
repeats itself. Yeah, well, apparently. Grow up, already, I tell her.

HAPPY HUNTING

When these women hold guns
there seems a correlation between size
of arms and size of clothing.

That one, with the shotgun,
wears only a bikini with her heavy,
high-laced boots.

The woman with the semi-automatic
wears a slip of a dress, rusty red,
as are her nylons.

Each of them has a rack
on her head—moose antlers
for the one pointing the pistol,

a buck's set of six-points
for the one propped with a rifle
on one hip, a hand on the other.

Their world is the most glorious
green, new-leaved and fresh, and
they won't move until you do.

VARANASI

Men here think it's funny to pull
a cap over my hair, laugh and call me
boy. This is what's left of my breasts
and hips six months into being host

to parasites, feasting on fat or female
hormones or whatever grants me curves.
I braid my hair tightly against my scalp,
layer thin cotton on thin cotton and shed

more than pounds and cells and grace
in this country, surprised at how quickly I can fall
asleep to the sound of dogs fighting. All around me,
men swagger and leer, strike poses

on riverbanks, strip stares into me on trains, hands
on crotches — theirs, mine — sticks in palms, held
loosely, raised at goats, chickens. I hate you
for them, for all the men you aren't but could be.

Tonight a woman says to me, "Good night.
God bless you. I love you." Silver slips off
my wrists and fingers, pinging stone streets
like chimed rain. I throw your ring into the Ganges,

a river so turbid and dark that nothing exists
beneath its surface, everything erased
except the bright blooms that cling to its skin.
Everything goes missing eventually.

ANITA

The wife serves you meals, three times a day. She stands beside you as you eat. When you ask, she tells you she has a degree in political science. You would like her to sit with you but she does not sit when she serves her mother-in-law. She does not sit when she serves her sister-in-law and her friends, nor does she when she serves her husband and their two sons. You are convinced by her and her mother-in-law to dress up in Anita's wedding sari. They wrap you in red and gold and send you out into the courtyard where her husband and his friends look at you and offer you drinks. You go back in and ask when the women will join you. Oh no, they said, that would not be right. The men are not family.

She would like you to go to a local restaurant and so you go with her husband and another man. They are pleasant and wait for you to laugh at their jokes. The husband does not drink much so that he can drive you to his home, where you stay in the guest cottage. In the driveway, he touches your thigh and tips his head and says, *Please* and when you say, *No*, he stops. You roll clothes into tight balls to fit in your backpack, leave while he is at work. You kiss Anita on the cheek and lean to hug the small boys goodbye.

FOR BETTER

The girls all wear black
bathing suits, face inward,
hips and bottoms visible, but not
their breasts, no lips or eyes.

The girls all wear black
bathing caps as well, the only difference
between them height or skin
colour. Can you begin

to separate one girl
from the other? To count
their legs or arms wound
round and round one another?

Look how tightly
they are huddled. How cold
their feet must be, bare
on that thick slab of ice.

When it breaks free,
it is called a floe. The girls
hold snug, don't think much
about its trajectory.

It must be heading south,
yes? Won't it all flow
south? It will be
warmer there.

Or are they confusing
south with downward?
For now, the water
is blessedly calm.

LUMBERJACK GIRL

Lumberjack girl, the forest is layered
in texture and sound, and there are more
shadows than you could cast yourself.

Close your eyes, pretend that there is someone
else here, out in the open, visible.
Keep what you carry behind your back—

no, lean it up behind the tree, then crawl
into that crack between rocks, show your
imagined audience shadow plays.

Wordless, you can damn philosophy
and slippery words that harden into forms,
sharp as blades or blunt as verse.

Lumberjack girl, this is just a story
you tell yourself. The forest is full
of trees. Your swing is strong and sure.

THAT FEELING

SHIELD, TOO

for Jill

I fall into step
with myself as I walk,

fallen leaves, fallow orchard or charred
earth underfoot from all that fall

burning, calves burn as I crest
the hill, calves become

cows in the fields, spring gone,
pickup truck seats sprung,

door gaping, mouth of coils
cut through vinyl, nothing

compared to this view, fog-heavy,
the lake leaden

far below. so far
we've logged so many

kilometres, logging roads
worth of ĸs, geese horning

their ᴠs into the sky,
walking I see all of it:

the crotch of fruit trees (real)
you across the road (in my mind)

ENDURE REASON

Let's say I am a horse, have the strength of a horse,
purebred. Let's pretend I am not the road
into which hooves pound and pound.

A hefty concept, gaining at a canter, a gallop, a trot,
increasing in weight and veracity over weeks,
months, from notion to soft tissue to bone.

But this is no gospel, this broad bend of skin, this flex
of tendon, this glossy animal riding my dreams,
unblinking, these smarting muscles, pulled.

And this isn't about pain, the rupture of water
hurled to the ground, the burst of inner river,
centred scorch radiating outward, just so.

Beyond the slick viscera, the sharp cries, the women
brimming around the bed, is the memory of weight,
first as I carried her then as she left me —

an instrument caught the reflection, baby held high
as though tiny and distant, one of Plato's perfect forms.
I was never the horse.

Whose strength I held, I don't know. We breed
them pure, our Boreas and Euros, so they can
endure this road, sully themselves silly with it.

IN ADVANCE OF LOSS

These are signs, warn believers, for the beginning
of the end, as if the universe hung from
a single unravelling thread.
—Aurian Haller

1.

She loses her lawn to the river
in yards—each day the length
of her body on shore is eaten
by rising water.

She sees birches bent across
the tangle of cottonwoods,
but knows no children
have swung them into the current—

first crows lined up, mocked their limbs
downward, then winter branded
the river until it froze, took the tips
of trees with it.

Now, the melt-water rises.
The wind's restive for something
with a little spring in it, for another form
off loss, ice shirking the shore.

2.

On what was once the outskirts of town,
they painted an oil drum in faux wood
then added parts to create a giant,
called him Mister Prince George.

When he revolts and dismounts his post
at the tourism info centre, Mr. PG high-steps
over trees and buildings until he reaches
a river intent on swallowing its own banks,

and walks in, a smile painted on his face.
He hungers for agency, the chance to be
pulled by the boot straps out of a river's spray
and into the stark, quivering sun.

3.

Driving, it is hard to see them
at first, the moose that lumber
out of snow banks, seeking respite,
a stretch of clear road. A few they miss

by a hair, one runs beside the truck so close
that she could slap its haunch out the window.
He dodges moose, she counts twenty-one,
snow spumed when each plunders the bank.

Now, she bare-knuckles the vestige
of winter. Blackbirds swarm, call out
to each other then launch off trees
on either side of the bloated river.

They fly toward each other, black arrows
marked with red and yellow. She turns away
so she won't see them collide, waves good bye
to Mr. PG as he floats away, his mouth full of foam.

MUSIC CLASS

Our children go to music class
at the same school I went to as a girl.
We make up a life

for them, decide what we will do each day,
what we will attempt to avoid. No TV. Instead
our children go to music class

while I wait in a room with other mothers, talk
about who grew up where and when and how
we make up a life

that makes sense in the retelling—why we are
where we are, what we do with our days, why
our children go to music class.

One of the women tells me about her husband
and I recognize his name. Sometimes, when
we make up a life,

we set aside the part when we were taken to the bush
and pushed down so that we can carry on while
our children go to music class.

His pickup polished, too clean, the headlights stark,
whitewashed the forest around us.
We make up a life

that we can handle. He cut the engine, told me
no one would hear, that it was too far to run. Now
our children go to music class;

then, he kept the radio on and I caught notes
in my throat when he forced himself into my mouth.
We make up a life,

sometimes on instinct. I kicked open the door
instead of biting down though, if I had, perhaps
our children wouldn't go to music class

together. It was too far to walk home
so I told him that if he gave me a ride
I would make up a life

in which I wouldn't mention him.
I don't say anything to his wife while
our children go to music class.

Instead, this becomes a refrain
that I write about, over and over, a way
I make up a life.

KICK A SMALL MOON

This is ours, and not ours, pass it on.
— Damian Rogers

Kick a small moon into the grass.
Giggle. Toss coins, lawn darts, desire
before they pin you to something.
Tear blank pages out of creased palms.

Be prepared for ignorance, teasing,
wounds, all exacted by you on you.
The future is an orphan, the dulcet
voice of radio tells you about its plight.

All the crayons are broken, the top
shelf of the cabinet is festooned
with tiny pills and sticky syrup
to make it okay, anyway.

There's a bear on the patio
and cubs curled into the tomato pots.
It takes us two days
to leave the house then

the sun presses down, crowns
our heads, knocks us on our arses,
forces light down our throats
till we're gutted by splendour.

Each season, we forget
the others, think this is it, this is
how it will be. We let go of the string
and the balloon floats away.

SOMEONE ELSE'S NORTH

We mark papers and hire sitters and drink to once upon
when we ranged north, spent summers in tents, biked
from Yukon to Alaska alone. Now, we apply for more grants,
allow ourselves to be stream-fed scraps of gossip.

Even in daydreams, we have the same décor: the animal skull
hung off-centre on a white wall, an iconic chair, vintage globe,
the taxidermied bird, for godsake — all ironic, or not.
Who is this *we*? you ask. Why am I roping you into this?

This is no mountain I've climbed alone, this dailiness,
these details. We are all complicit. A friend closes a door
behind a grad student and you don't say anything, then or later.
Before we documented everything, I had nothing but memory

to mark my solo ascents. Halfway up Montana Mountain,
I heard the rasp of breath first then hooves severed
the icy skein of snow before I looked up from my climb
to catch the sidelong glance of a caribou as it ran by.

I can see its large, glossy eyeball roll toward me,
hear the whir of insects alighting on my exposed skin
until I climbed high enough that I was through them.
That is someone else's north now; my polestar shifting

as my compass trembles like a pulse. Friends appear
onscreen, well-linked and adorned with witticisms.
Our time-lines flicker, backlit. We're all amateurs —
our history, our cartography as looped and twisted as string.

DISRESPECTING GRAVITY

This revolution is over
and I must live irrespective
of gravity
and galaxies colliding
—Barbara Coupé

Think about how tree trunks split, the space
between them. You go to bed
requesting me, generally, my heat

more specifically, or was it vice versa?
Can love do this—tip the canoe,
trap me in a vacuum of lip

and water surface? Let's sleep now,
without respecting gravity or much
beyond the obvious.

I come up for air, hit my head
on the underbelly of the boat.
You pull me out.

Lake water finds ways to run off
and return, the cycle so complete
we can swim in it. Every morning,

last night's revoltion of the earth is over
and beginning again. We continue to live
heedless of gravity, galaxies colliding.

DECADENT NUT ORCHARD

Decadent: marked by decay or decline

Classicism is the subordination of the parts to the whole; decadence is the subordination of the whole to the parts.
—Oscar Wilde

When we move, winter comes on slowly as though fall
waits for us to change seasons, trees bare, fields open.

Most things in storage, we carry what we can, trip
with baby or toddler underfoot, so yielding, open.

We rent before finding a place we can throw down
something as tangled and conjoined as roots, revealed.

We walk the property—you stop, name things, stumble
on the Latin, notice what's overgrown, concealed, open.

The fence needs repair, south corner rotted and crumbling.
On the other side a nut orchard, ladders against trees open.

The orchard decadent, past prime—stray nuts may fall,
exposed when weeds are trimmed, ground uncovered.

Why the sprung ladders? Who climbs them, risks slipping?
Trees have to be pruned, dead cut back, trunks left open.

I'm not so different, post-babies, as my mental state skids
off course yet still heaves uneven verse, stunted yet open.

Is this decadence? On whom does the responsibility fall
to prune the branches that are most cloying, vulnerable?

It's up to me, I guess, to decide what to edit though I fall
for every surge of deceptive fecundity, mind dogged, open.

Up for suggestions, I'm a flowering bush one day, dropping
blossoms, then a decaying tree distorting itself, roots open.

Is that what this is? A kind of decadent swirl of descent
into tawdry, simple metaphor? I'm so bloody guileless —

in first person or third, a tree or an orchard of nuts falling
to the ground heavily enough to crack shells, split fruit open.

LATE

Give me obituaries, birth announcements —
I'll imagine a life, analyze a name in terms
of style, contemporary or classic, compatibility
with siblings and spouses. I'll find something
to criticize, something to praise, new and gone alike.

The women, their lives canned and quilted, baked
into the memories of their children, and I wonder:
Really? Is that all those left behind chose to record?
I love a canned peach but, good Lord, if anyone mentions
mine when I am dead, my time was not well spent.

I am desperate for something other than embroidery
and pie. If you could please mention how well
I loved that would be enough. How loudly
we laughed, hollered, crashed and rolled about,
each of you loving the pants off my heart.

Can this be my obituary? Can we have more
children? I've got a shortlist of their names chosen.
There is so much more I want to do, so much
more I want to write, but I should sleep now.
It's late.

BITE MARKS

You don't want to leave bite marks
on a man's shoulder to have another
woman notice them. His shirt
should not have been off. It wasn't
that hot. She slept with him

first, you were with another before
her, your swaps separated by months
then weeks. What kind of travelling
companion was she, dressed like you,
journaling just as furiously?

You said goodbye to each other in India,
except you couldn't say it, one of you
in a silent retreat, the other withdrawing
out of the country. It was Valentine's Day.
Years later, drunk, she tells you she was in love

with you, briefly, foolishly, the way those things
happened. Years after that, you remember
when you switched lovers, those hypothetical
same-sex affairs, but you can't quite
imagine any of that anymore.

You feel old enough to know what it's like
when both men and women stop looking.
You buy boxes of apples from the orchard,
sink your teeth into the skin, leave them
unfinished, souring in air.

THANKSGIVING

Paul forgets to close the door
when he pees and I walk by,
see those cheeks and want
to give him a quick slap.

He's all about hand-eye
coordination, trained for years
on video games for a shot
at something airborne and American

—what, I'm not entirely sure.
Nothing more than accidental
travelling companions, we share
not even a room but a hostel

in a country that is neither of ours.
This holiday is observed only
for our benefit. At home we celebrate
on different days but our two countries

are equally comfortable with the feigned
enthusiasm of others to put things on
for us; versions of our emblems
makeshift, half-arsed but genuine.

Paul's been accepted. This is his
last hoorah before deployment.
I don't approve of anything
except his body, the way

he holds it away from me,
safe-guarding all sensations,
saving reflexes for rapid fire. I am left
unsated as conversation veers toward politics.

That September in New York
has not yet happened. No rerun of storm
in the desert just fine grains of sand
kicked up into phosphorescence

around our ankles
and a decorative gourd
that he keeps stroking
as though to punctuate speech.

TWO GIRLS, REFRACTED

In the parked truck, there is only so long
she can stay quiet. She grips the steering wheel, grinning.
Pigtails pull each corner of her mouth, smile bright,

the way the sun winks off the gleam of the hood.
Her T-shirt announces nothing except
perhaps, nine years old—yeah, what else?

When she can't take it any longer, she jumps,
mouth covered to suppress yelps of glee,
tugs at her papa's ear, retreats into the truck.

Hair matted into a brown nest, another girl
inside the diner, clothes as pink as fingertips, tongues—
thwack-thwack a jump rope against floor.

Rhythm only comes in good ways for these girls now,
bodies quick, hearts thumping as
they lead the march then beat a safe retreat.

They lead the march then beat a safe retreat,
bodies quick, hearts thumping as
rhythm only comes in good ways for these girls now,

thwack-thwack a jump rope against floor
inside the diner. Clothes as pink as fingertips, tongues.
Hair matted into a brown nest, another girl

tugs at her papa's ear, retreats into the truck,
mouth covered to suppress yelps of glee.
When she can't take it any longer, she jumps.

Perhaps nine years old. Yeah, what else?
Her T-shirt announces nothing except
the way the sun winks off the gleam of the hood.

Pigtails pull each corner of her mouth, smile bright.
She can stay quiet. She grips the steering wheel, grinning
in the parked truck. There is only so long.

TWO OR MORE STORIES: A SPLIT GHAZAL

I drive the kids to preschool past two snow-covered tennis courts.
Sometimes, there are people at the bus stop, the cue split in two:

those who seem fine, those who might be from a halfway house
near here. They gesture and mutter, as though they're split into two

different people, each half arguing with the other. I see your brother,
once the region's best tennis player until the year when he split in two,

though that's a dated and simplified explanation, you once told me.
It took years for diagnosis and wasn't as simple as being split in two—

the older brother you adored and the one you feared. The strain
may have caused your mother's early stroke which split her in two,

the taut coil of woman who snapped and yelled and her dual self
who unravelled and cracked with sexual innuendo. Split in two,

just like I am—she and I share a birthday, born under the sign of twins.
You and I broke up, the phrase implying more than being split in two—

rather, space between the shards of the life lived, the one longed for.
In two years, I would marry and two after that I would be split in two

by the birth of my first child, his labour straddling two days before
he opened me as light bled into the dawn of my birthday, split in two,

now mine and his. Childbirth tore me open but I'm beyond broken,
more a puzzle with so many pieces that I can't simply be split in two.

I was with my husband and kids on the ski hill when I remembered
a run with you and there you were, in the present, past split in two:

the one that ended, the one that carried on down parallel courses.
You were with your brother and his wide grin split his face in two.

It was winter and we were insulated in down, flanked by family,
but part of me was back in that summer, under a tree, split in two.

The third person is always me, the poet. I just want to feel the joy
of playing the ball so the net that splits the court in two disappears.

SUBURBAN POOLSIDE, IMAGINED

I had a sister, lived in the suburbs —
in my dreams, sister, in my dreams!
Reality: one brother, field of stubble.

Even in dreams that sister
had a plain face — and, oh, how little
she revealed on the surface.

She would raise her arms
and, without visible effort, slip
herself into the backyard pool, her dive

faultless. I would sit on the edge,
feet submerged, and my brother
would appear to say,

"I don't feel like swimming."
I agreed. Always, in dreams, I would
agree. Around us, insects

caught air in their wings,
tore at it with sound. My sister
emerged, dripping

as I woke, sheets soaked again,
baseboard heater cranked, window
wide open, heat pulsing

out of the house. A coyote
on the road slowed, raised its snout
to the smell of a girl shifting in her sleep.

THAT FEELING

Run your body through the lake —
morning, afternoon or evening, make it
    once a day, at least once.

Sit down, I'll make you a drink.
Gin and tonic? Rye and coke? How
are you feeling — urbane? Rugged?

Please, go ahead — tremble, stain
the dock like the last minutes of a fish, open
    your mouth, gape, tongue agog.

I'll take care of the kids. Let me open
the door so you can hear her lilting scales on piano.
Oh, look! He's reading Derrida already!

Tilt your head. Drink the sky like berry-filled
birds that wheel in air and then drop, drunk
into bushes again; they want more.

Garden tools and knives can look the same
colour as the ground until it rains and the sun shines.
    Then they glint. We should move those.

A boat tears a strip down the lake, sears us with sound.
I'm considering getting one of those retro-style swimsuits
with missiles for breasts. What do you think?

I guess that the way we shudder when we swallow
    and swallow again shakes us open to that sweet
sense of something else. That feeling, I mean.

GIRL AT THE END OF THE DRIVE

The sound comes from the end of the drive
as you are getting ready for bed, light
still on. Her calls stop you, hand
hovering near your throat, body
tight. A woman's screams, shrill, a heavy
jolt in your blood. Your mind circles

around what to do, echo of her shrieks circle
the house, an engine wails, a car drives
away and you are left to imagine somebody
left on the edge of the property, retreating headlights.
You open curtains, listen to nothing but heavy
silence, the phone already in your hand.

You tell the dispatcher what you heard, hand
it over to the police, hope they will circle
the neighbourhood, make sure nobody
can still be harmed. You hear the car driving
away, the retch of its muffler. You turn out the light
but can't sleep, her imagined presence outside so heavy

it muffles any peace required for rest, heavy
though sleep might come. An officer phones and your hand
shakes as he asks if you can identify the car. The light
isn't good, you say, trees a thick circle
around the house, you could only hear someone drive
away as her screams ricocheted, rocked your own body,

as though ripped from your throat, your body
hers, left down a dark street, each house behind heavy
trees, cellphone in the car that you both hear him drive
away. You each fold in on yourselves, faces in hands,
throats coarse, keep quiet now so he will not circle
back, change his mind about leaving, go all the way, light

into her, an imagined you, until there is nothing left, no light,
just leaden sky, circle of black trees, rough road. Just her body,
yours, separated by a stretch of driveway, fear circling
through each of you at different angles, yours heavy
with the distress of not knowing, hers weighted with the hand
that struck her, the hand that traced her arm so lightly on that first drive

into the last light of a summer evening, desire heavy
in the car between them, bodies light in each other's hands
as they circled skin, touched each other the whole long sweet drive.

PINHOLE CAMERA : : POSTWAR PRAIRIE

As a girl, her world looked better
upside down. Head between legs
she set it straight—sky solid, ground brilliant.

Inverted, it became clear, exposed:
her father's boot parted fields, an insect marched
up her leg, mother in the sky. Distance obscured,

light tumbled over ankles, length
shuttered off her own reflection.
When it was too much, she

blackened the room, left a hole—
the world would shine, the world would shine.
Left a hole, blackened the room

when it was too much. She
shuttered off her own reflection,
light tumbled over ankles, length

up her leg. Mother in the sky, distance obscured,
her father's boot parted fields, an insect marched,
inverted. It was clear, exposed—

she set it straight. Sky solid, ground brilliant
upside down, head between legs.
As a girl, her world looked better.

THE TRUTH WILL WEAR YOU OUT

Although there was no reason to think ourselves special,
there was also little reason to assume the neighbourhood was littered
with dead deer. Our fawn and how many others? Four or five or six,

went local legend, followed by as many how and when and why
lines of inquiry but shapes couldn't be drawn, no diagram
to illustrate the truth about our time, when we would all succumb

to something or other. I was already keeping the kids in
because of bears; rumour of cougars wouldn't change much.
It was that season, the one when we started to watch TV

again, or replayed our own past dramas to dull effect, hoping
always for epiphany, wore ourselves out instead, dragged each other
to bed, the points on your antlers as sharp as my claws.

If you're a buck and I'm a mountain lion, perhaps we're evenly matched
to take on all of this. Come on, let's be fierce together, wildly protective
of our brood, falling through sky locked in a thorny embrace.

HARD-WON

Milk pumped into bags, cycles
from cold pack to freezer to fridge to bottle.
I'm told the baby doesn't always refuse,
has a fickle relationship with disembodiment.

My body wants the baby, wants the baby
bad, breasts hard and sore, release far more
of a hassle without her, the apparatus awkward,
cold. We each carry something that smells

like each other, the baby and I. A comfort
for her, a cue for my body to produce food
in her absence. I can pump with one hand,
write with the other, though both wrists cramp.

I plug seventies rock ballads into my ears and shake
out my arms. Door closed, blinds drawn, bottled milk
still warm, I dance, a baby blanket cut in two
the thing I clutch as I let out a mute howl

of lip-synced mania. I'm crazy for all of this—you,
the kids, the work, the words—and I can
pack it all away before the next student
arrives for his appointment.

On the drive home, silhouettes of tin boats are cut out
of the lake's refracted light and time is a lyric
repeated: those old guys fishing, their trucks
and trailers left on the side of the highway.

Days loll beneath them, slap against the side
of the boat as I pass, glance in the rearview mirror
to make sure I've remembered the milk,
packed in ice, poems written in hopes that it keeps.

A NEW KIND OF FIRE

We are recently domesticated, still surprised
how the shape and heat of our fear
has shifted and followed us, sullied
the house with the smell
of meat, metal, wet cotton.

Our fright was once reserved
for fiercer things: being alone
on mountains cloistered in fog,
rides snagged from road sides, currents
that cut our ankles with their hidden edge.

Danger now loiters in each split level,
throws curveballs down every cul-de-sac,
ricochets off garage doors, is speared
on the tips of fences.

But no, that's not it. It's us.
We don't fear the trappings,
we fear ourselves in them. It's okay —

we can still laugh about it,
backyards splayed with mottled shade,
drinks hard enough to wait until noon, soft enough
to seem harmless. Our children barefoot

in grass speckled with broken glass, unseen,
light sliced on imagined edges.

Our husbands joke about the barbecue,
its unpredictability, and we see fireballs
like second suns or constellations of searing new stars
dotting backyards, our subdivision charted in heat.

MIGRATORY PATHS

We look at the world once, in childhood.
The rest is memory.
—Louise Glück

Stencil silhouettes of birds
to windows. When the real things
strike the glass, remember their patterns
of flight have nothing to do with you, your offspring
gap-mouthed minnows behind the pane.

The consolation of biology: everything
has a use, appetite, expiration. The machinations
of songs and photographs, our sheets, littered
inboxes of computers—all gnash gears,
endeavour to slow decay but it travels

the body like blood, quickens us. It is what
lifts off in the moment before falling
asleep: the light we release, percolate with panic,
mouth slack, a breach opening
into a migratory world that etches paths
across our palms, rings empty cups,
leaves the lawn dappled with feathers.

Birds repeat themselves, declare victory
in the sky seasonally while below arteries
are jellied with fish eggs that our daughter
pops between finger and thumb.

We are tokens of cellular recall laddered
through spines and follicles, spectres
of desire for variation, as though we could
offer the role of tree or harbour for decades,
promise roots, branches, tributaries.

Look, we say, here is the world!
You'll see it all once; the rest is memory.

STRUNG

Each morning might be a dull emergency —
small alarms of pine siskins startled by daylight,
the children calling our names like a mantra.

Did I tell you? I saw light push through marble
at the Taj Mahal once. I felt good about that
then tasted the wreck of myself in a thick drink

bought for a rupee on a holy night, felt too far
from a ticket office that could sell me
the promise of the idea of home.

That was all so long ago and we are full of unmet sleep,
our bathing suits still wet. The kids reek of lake
when I sneak into their room to breathe them.

We are here, we made it and we're still smarting
from the most recent move, hardwired for change,
trip-wired over each other. When the kids sleep,

we drink to our ledges, the ways we each find our way
down. I guess at them in the dark, blinking lights
on clock, computer, phone charger no landing strip

to mark direction. Instead they cast constellations
through the room; imagined lines bisect space
and we are inert, cagey of ways we could set things off,

our moods, their night-waking. Forget the kids —
they sleep while I'm strung on night, the salvage
of lean latitude, this time, alone in the dark.

Let's call this our kingdom, this sky our very own,
or claim the way it is littered with stars, smudged clusters
as scattered as we are. As small, as bright.

BOLT

The days are peppered with rapid-fire reports
of threats, possible harm in the form of mushrooms
or blades or the black bloom of a stranger's heart pounding.

My mind shutters through glowing screens, searching
for the next hit. I avoid television but the radio follows me
from room to car, spliced into equal parts dire, hopeful, wise.

I want radio-free transport, hooves on gravel, heat
of a body to ride, not the boys I bucked off
me on the bench seats of pickups. Not the men

I wished I'd shucked like bad outfits or temporary jobs.
Not even the body of the man I married when I wanted
the smell of the back of his neck forever—not him,

but this horse on a northern back road that I ride straight
for a moose stamped on the crest of the hill like a figment
of Canadiana. The horse bolts. Once, I would have let go,

would have thought the crack of helmet, broken clavicle worth
a moment of air; would have felt ready for my body to forget
its weight, ready to remember it when the road came up heavy to
        meet me.

Now, I hold on. I learn this about horses: they always find their way
back to the stable. Mine gallops all the way there, my body clenched
        around it.
I dismount and walk to the car, gingerly, leave space between my legs.

The radio wavers in and out as I punch through ranges
of reception on the drive home. Advisories advise boiled water,
the river roils, our war dead are tallied but I don't hear the number.

YOUNG WOMAN DRIVING AT NIGHT

At night the young woman would drive
herself round the twist in her parents'
sedan, cider-jazzed limbs doing the steering,
corners interpreted with a loose jig of give
and seize, rush of creek water symphonic
through windows, skin light-flecked,
the fantastic larvae of all her tomorrows
curled and growing; she drove
herself, the road was narrow
and it curved and it kept going
as long as she did.

NOTES

"To Do:" was inspired by "Their Vocal Soul Din" by Gale Nelson.

"Fissure & Flood" is the second poem I've written in response to Alex Boyd's "Two Thirteen Line Poems on Why We Need a New Poem."

"The Kind of Weather I Have" is in response David Huddle's poem "The Weather."

"Shield, Too" is out walking with Gillian Wigmore's poem "Shield."

"In Advance of Loss" is a conversation with Aurian Haller about the ambivalence of water and sump pump hearts.

The epigraph from "Kick a Small Moon" is from Damian Roger's "Museum of Tomorrow," a poem that laughs as it kicks a sphere.

The epigraph from "Disrespecting Gravity" is from Barbara Coupé's "Irrespective."

The last line of "That Feeling" is from Simon Armitage's "It Ain't What You Do, It's What It Does to You."

The epigraph from "Migratory Paths" is from Louise Glück's "Nostos," as is the idea of promising the role of tree for decades.

"Slightly Creepy Camping Site," "Boy Scouts," "For Better," "Lumberjack Girl" and "Happy Hunting" were inspired by the work of visual artist, Karin Bos, as it appears in the book *A Trip to the Countryside* (Karin Bos, Netherlands, 2009).

"Fairytales for Loss," "Among Apologies," "We Were Reasoning Wildly," "Endure Reason," "In Advance of Loss" and "The Truth Will Wear You Out" were inspired by the work of visual artist Theresa Sapergia, as it appears in the catalogue *Anthems of Life Interrupted* for an exhibition of the same name at the Two Rivers Gallery in Prince George, BC (2009).

ACKNOWLEDGEMENTS

Early versions of some of these poems appeared in *Arc*, *The Geographical Review*, *Canadian Literature*, *Event*, *Grain*, *PRISM international*, *The Malahat Review* and *The New Quarterly* and were anthologized in *Force Field: 77 Women Poets of British Columbia* (Mother Tongue), *Naked in Academe: Celebrating 50 Years of Creative Writing at UBC* (McClelland & Stewart/Random House of Canada) and *Unfurled: Collected Poetry of Northern BC Women* (Cailtin Press). My sincere thanks to the editors of each.

A selection of these poems was published in a limited-edition chapbook, *This Glossy Animal*, by Baseline Press. Thank you to Karen Schindler for finding and shaping the work into a beautiful little book.

Thank you to visual artists Karin Bos and Theresa Sapergia whose work had a strong impact on me, emotionally and conceptually. A big thanks to Theresa Sapergia for the use of a detail from *We Were Reasoning Wildly*, as well as to Carleton Wilson for the striking cover design.

Thank you, Silas White, for taking this trip as my editor for the third time. Your sharp eye, keen ear and patience make the ride smoother. Thanks to everyone at Nightwood Editions and Harbour Publishing for all you do for writers, readers and book culture.

I'm so grateful to those who saw these poems at various stages and nudged them along—Marita Dachsel, Jason Dewinetz, Jennica Harper, Jake Kennedy, Nancy Lee and Gillian Wigmore. Thank you to my family, especially to Amalia, Jonah and Aaron Deans. You are each part of these poems, in some way, and my writing life thrives, in part, because of each of you.

Photo Credit: Tracey Nearmy

Laisha Rosnau is the author of the best-selling novel *The Sudden Weight of Snow* (McClelland & Stewart) and the Nightwood Editions poetry collections *Lousy Explorers*, nominated for the Pat Lowther Award, and *Notes on Leaving*, which won the Acorn–Plantos People's Poetry Prize. Rosnau lives in Coldstream, BC, where she and her family are resident caretakers of Bishop Wild Bird Sanctuary.